LEADERS
Gabby Douglas

BY J.P. MILLER
ILLUSTRATED BY
DAVID WILKERSON

Reader Choice Title

Rourke

ROURKE'S SCHOOL to HOME CONNECTIONS

BEFORE AND DURING READING ACTIVITIES

Before Reading: *Building Background Knowledge and Vocabulary*

Building background knowledge can help children process new information and build upon what they already know. Before reading a book, it is important to tap into what children already know about the topic. This will help them develop their vocabulary and increase their reading comprehension.

Questions and Activities to Build Background Knowledge:

1. Look at the front cover of the book and read the title. What do you think this book will be about?
2. What do you already know about this topic?
3. Take a book walk and skim the pages. Look at the table of contents, photographs, captions, and bold words. Did these text features give you any information or predictions about what you will read in this book?

Vocabulary: *Vocabulary Is Key to Reading Comprehension*

Use the following directions to prompt a conversation about each word.

- Read the vocabulary words.
- What comes to mind when you see each word?
- What do you think each word means?

Vocabulary Words:
- enrolled
- gymnastics
- national
- recreational
- retired
- routine
- siblings
- vision

During Reading: *Reading for Meaning and Understanding*

To achieve deep comprehension of a book, children are encouraged to use close reading strategies. During reading, it is important to have children stop and make connections. These connections result in deeper analysis and understanding of a book.

Close Reading a Text

During reading, have children stop and talk about the following:

- Any confusing parts
- Any unknown words
- Text to text, text to self, text to world connections
- The main idea in each chapter or heading

Encourage children to use context clues to determine the meaning of any unknown words. These strategies will help children learn to analyze the text more thoroughly as they read.

When you are finished reading this book, turn to the next-to-last page for **Text-Dependent Questions** and an **Extension Activity**.

TABLE OF CONTENTS

BORN A GYMNAST 4

GOAL TO GET THE GOLD 8

A HERO'S WELCOME 14

TIME LINE 21

GLOSSARY 22

INDEX 23

TEXT-DEPENDENT QUESTIONS 23

EXTENSION ACTIVITY 23

ABOUT THE AUTHOR
AND ILLUSTRATOR 24

BORN A GYMNAST

Do you have a **vision** for your life? What is it? How will you do it? Gabby Douglas made plans to be an Olympic athlete. She is a leader in women's **gymnastics**.

All eyes were on the scoreboard. Gabby looked too. The crowd cheered and applauded. She had completed her **routine** in the women's gymnastics individual all-around at the 2012 London Olympics. She waited to see if she won.

"It's a Gabby Gold!" the announcer exclaimed.

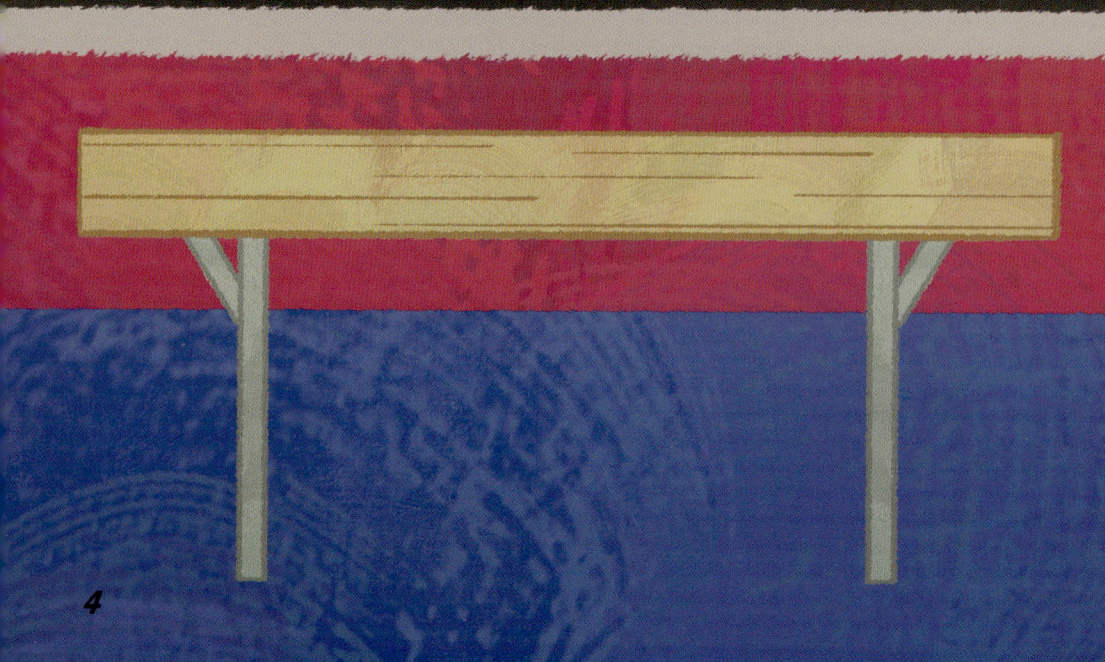

GYMNASTICS ALL-AROUND COMPETITION

The all-around is where a gymnast competes in four events: the vault, uneven bars, balance beam, and floor exercises. The gymnast with the highest combined score across all events is the winner. In the case of the Olympics, not all gymnasts compete in the all-around.

Gabby had dreamed of that moment her whole life. Even as a baby, Gabby seemed to be preparing for an Olympic career. She had heard stories of how she climbed out of her crib.

She loved playing with her older sister Arielle. The nine-year-old showed young Gabby how to do cartwheels, handstands, splits, and more. She was amazed how fast Gabby caught on. Arielle talked their mother into putting Gabby in gymnastics classes.

7

GOAL TO GET THE GOLD

The door to Gymstrada Gymnastics swung open. Six-year-old Gabby darted past her mother and **siblings** and went straight to the mats. She wanted to start classes at once.

The gym was busy. Students were doing

tuck jumps on the trampoline...
...back flips on the balance beam...
...and underswings on the uneven bars.

"Do I get to come back?" Gabby asked as they were leaving. The answer was yes. Her mother had **enrolled** all four of her children in gymnastics lessons that day.

Gabby worked hard. She learned to use all the equipment. Her coach was surprised by her skills. He asked if Gabby could move to advanced lessons.

Gabby moved up from **recreational** classes to Level 4. She could now compete against others. She competed in the Virginia State Championships as a Level 4 all-around gymnast. She won the gold medal. Some said she was great like Olympic gymnast Dominque Dawes. Gabby had not heard of her, so she looked her up on social media. Dominque inspired Gabby. She set a goal to win the gold at the London Summer Olympics.

With this hope, Gabby competed in the US Classic in Houston, Texas. It was her first time performing at the **national** level. She placed 10th in the all-around rankings. Gabby knew she could do better.

HOW TO BECOME A LEVEL-4 GYMNAST
Level 4 is the first level of competition in gymnastics. The gymnast must be at least seven years old and meet all requirements. Requirements include specific skills on the vault, balance beam, uneven bars, and floor routines.

If Gabby was going to win Olympic gold, she knew she had to have the best coach. Even if it meant moving thousands of miles from her family to Des Moines, Iowa. Coach Liang Chow had coached others and they won gold medals. Gabby was sure he could do the same for her.

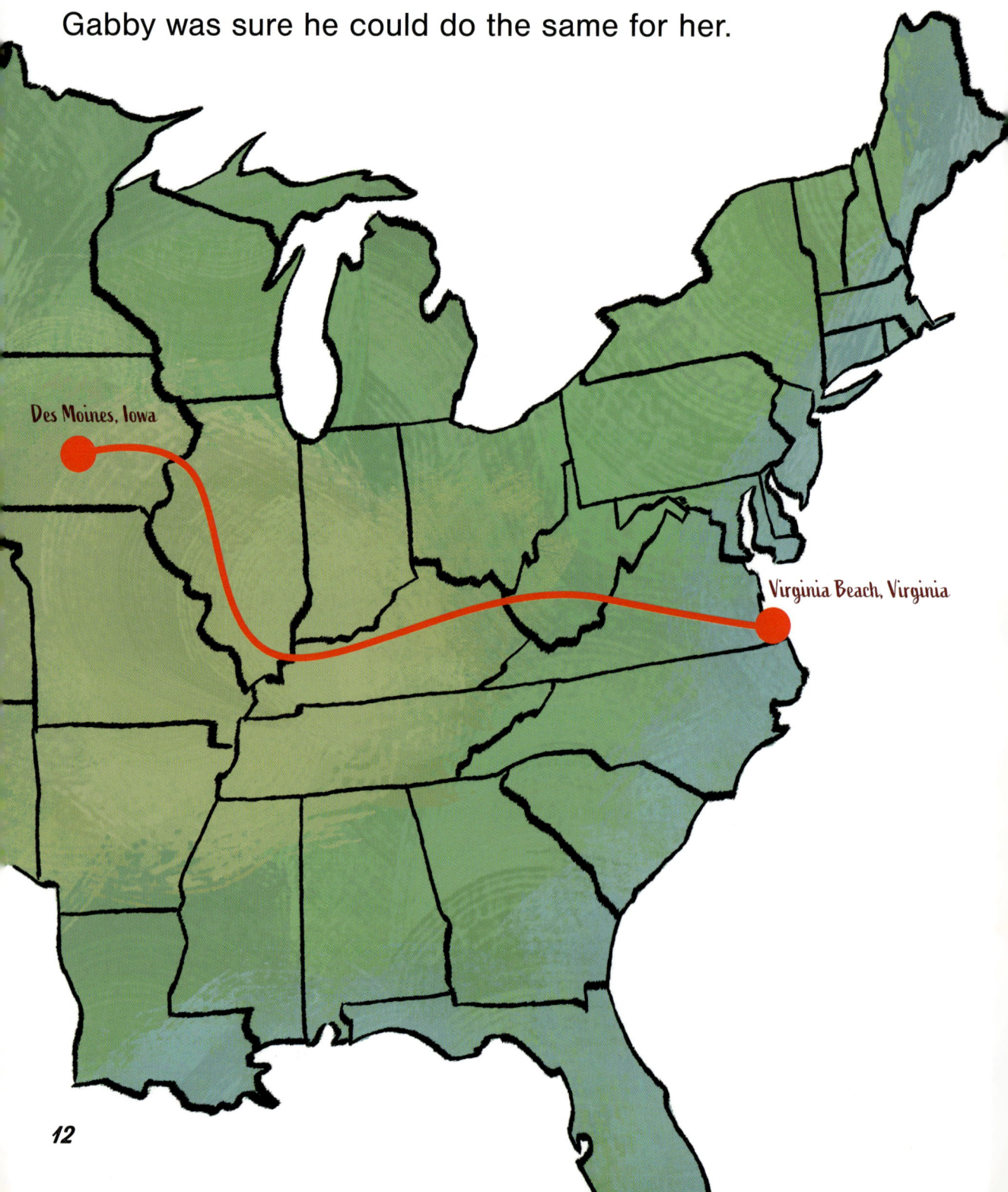

Gabby lived with Travis and Missy Parton for 22 months while she trained in Iowa. They were her sponsor family. In her family Gabby was the youngest. She enjoyed being the oldest in the Parton Family.

A HERO'S WELCOME

Gabby flipped and danced her way into homes around the world with her performance at the London 2012 Olympics. She was the first US woman gymnast to win a gold medal in both the individual and team all-around. She was also the first African American to do so.

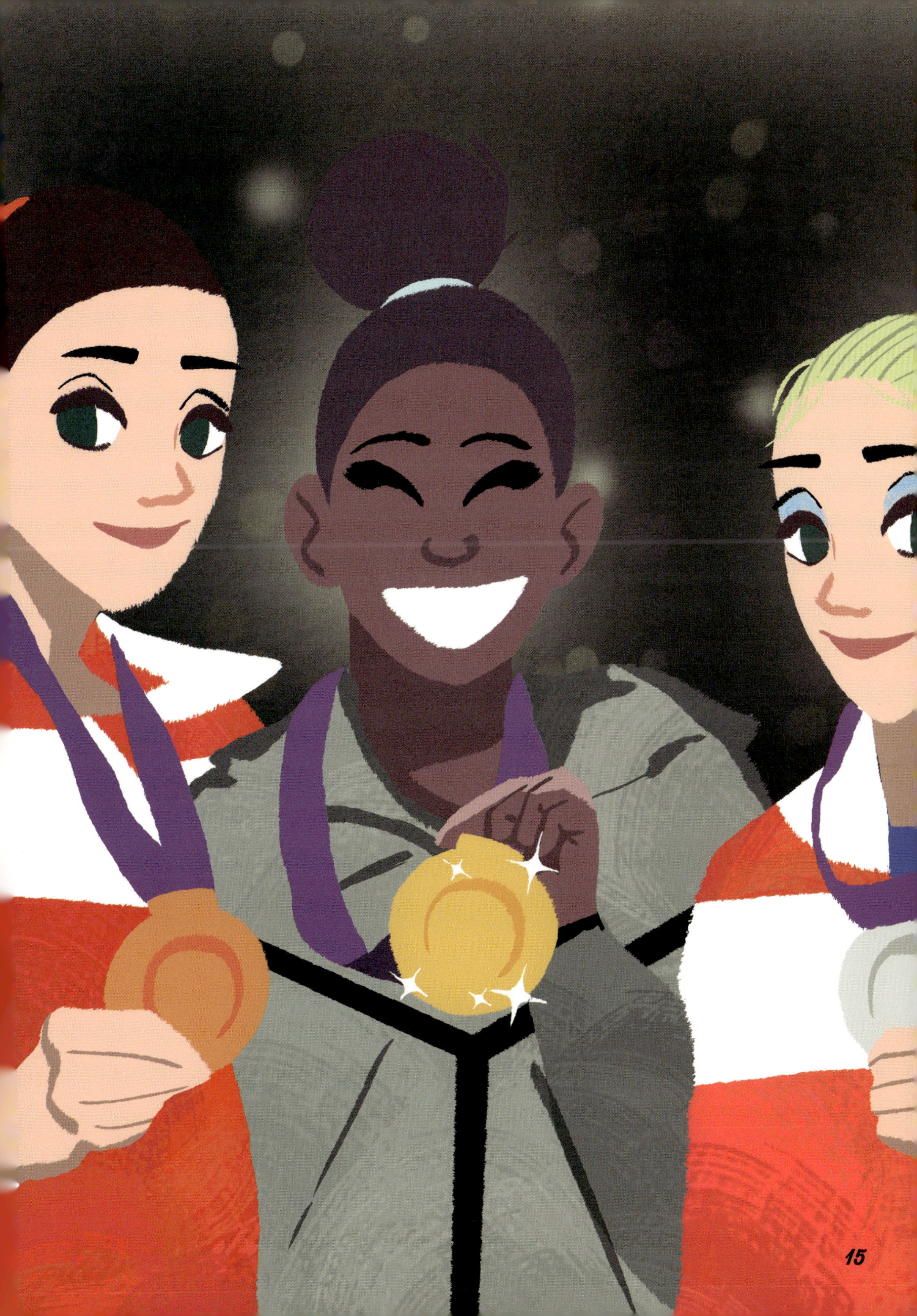

Gabby came home a hero. She was on the box of Kellogg's Corn Flakes and was on a lot of talk shows. A movie called *The Gabby Douglas Story* was made about her life in 2014. In 2015, a reality show called *Douglas Family Gold* was created about Gabby and her family.

17

Gabby also released her book, *Grace, Gold, & Glory: My Leap of Faith*. But more than anything, the fifteen-year-old world champion simply wanted her driver's license.

In 2016, Gabby made it to the Olympics again. She was one of the "Final Five" who won gold in the team all-around in Rio de Janeiro. The team went on a city-to-city tour when they got back to the US.

FINAL FIVE

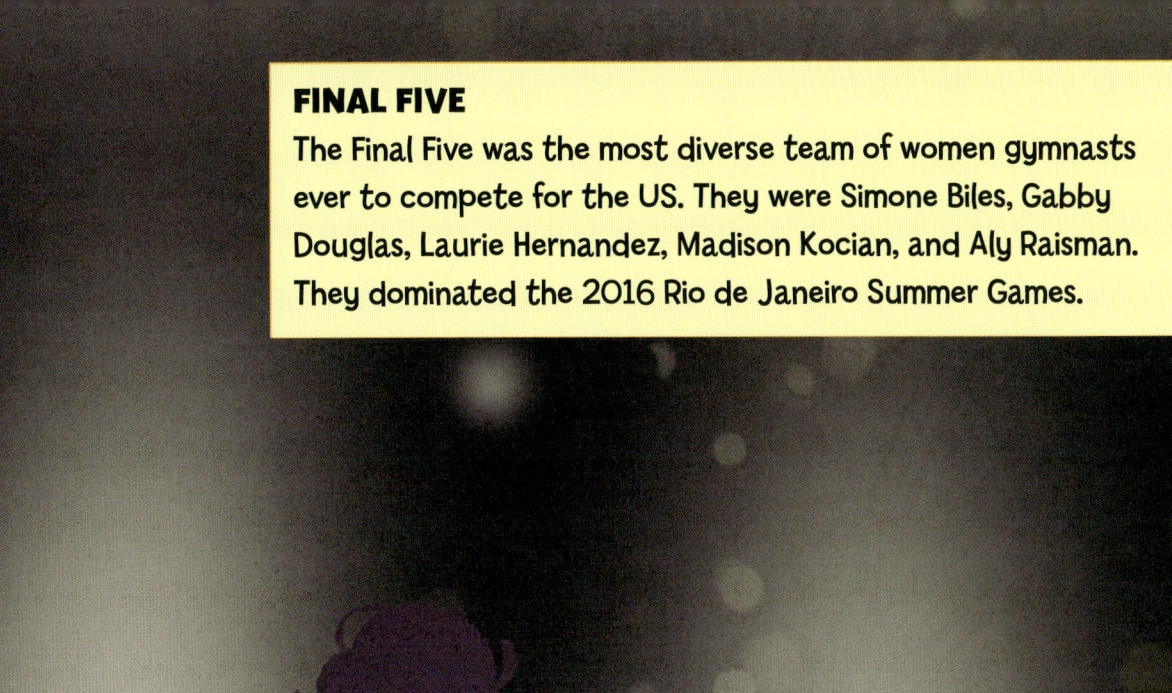

The Final Five was the most diverse team of women gymnasts ever to compete for the US. They were Simone Biles, Gabby Douglas, Laurie Hernandez, Madison Kocian, and Aly Raisman. They dominated the 2016 Rio de Janeiro Summer Games.

Gabby Douglas **retired** from gymnastics in 2016. In 2021, she was on the variety show *The Masked Dancer,* where she was disguised as a character called Cotton Candy. She competed against other stars in a dance competition. Gabby won!

> "Train hard, dream big, just believe."
> –Gabby Douglas

TIME LINE

1995 Gabrielle "Gabby" Douglas is born on December 31st to Natalie Hawkins Douglas and Timothy Douglas in Newport News, Virginia.

1998 At age three, Gabby is first introduced to cartwheels and other gymnastic skills by her nine-year-old sister Arielle.

2002 Gabby and her siblings are enrolled in classes at Gymstrada Gymnastics.

2004 Gabby wins the Level 4 all-around gymnastics competition and becomes the Virginia State Champion.

2008 Gabby competes in the US Classic in Houston, Texas. It is her national debut. She places 10th in all-around rankings. Gabby moves to Des Moines, Iowa to be coached by Liang Chow of Chow's Gymnastics & Dance Institute. The Parton family is her sponsor family for 22 months.

2012 Gabby competes in the London Summer Olympics. She is the second African American to ever make the gymnastics team and the first African American to win gold medals in the team and individual and all-around events. She also releases her book *Grace, Gold, and Glory: My Leap of Faith*.

2013 Gabby releases her book *Raising the Bar*.

2014 *The Gabby Douglas Story* movie airs on the Lifetime channel.

2015 *Douglas Family Gold* airs on the Oxygen channel.

2016 Gabby competes in the Rio de Janeiro Summer Olympics.

2020 Gabby participates in the FOX network hit variety show *The Masked Dancer* as Cotton Candy and wins.

GLOSSARY

enrolled (en-ROHLD): to have registered as a student or member of something

gymnastics (jim-NAS-tiks): physical exercises, often performed on equipment such as ropes or parallel bars, involving flexibility, strength, balance, and coordination

national (NASH-uh-nuhl): of, having to do with, or shared by a whole nation

recreational (rek-ree-AY-shuhn-uhl): relating to an activity done in your spare time for fun

retired (ri-TIRE-urd): to have stopped working

routine (roo-TEEN): a worked-out part of an entertainment or sport contest that may be repeated

siblings (SIB-lings): brothers or sisters

vision (VIZH-uhn): something that you imagine or dream about

INDEX

balance 5, 8, 11
disguised 20
equipment 9
inspired 10
Level 4 10, 11
performance 14
social media 10
sponsor family 13

TEXT-DEPENDENT QUESTIONS

1. What does it mean to be Level 4 in gymnastics?
2. Who first noticed that Gabby was good at gymnastics?
3. What is an all-around competition?
4. What Olympic gymnast was Gabby compared to?
5. How old was Gabby when she won her first Olympic gold medal?

EXTENSION ACTIVITY

Create a vision board! Find a quiet space and think about what you want to do in the next year. Write your goals down on a piece of paper. Using a computer with a printer or magazines and newspapers, find images that represent what you want to do and cut them out. Use a corkboard or poster board and attach your images to it. Add personal touches to your vision board by writing or drawing on the images. Hang your vision board where you can see it and be reminded to do the things you planned.

ABOUT THE AUTHOR

J.P. Miller Growing up, J.P. Miller loved reading stories that she could become immersed in. As a writer, she enjoys doing the same for her readers. Through the gift of storytelling, she is able to bring little- and well-known people and events in African American history to life for young readers. She hopes that her stories will augment the classroom experience and inspire her readers. J.P. lives in metro Atlanta and is the author of the *Careers in the US Military* and *Black Stories Matter* series. J.P. is the winner of the 2021 Black Authors Matter Award sponsored by the National Black Book Festival.

ABOUT THE ILLUSTRATOR

David Wilkerson was born in Denver, CO and is currently based in Maryland. He developed a love for illustration during his high school years. His career began in the animation industry, working as a character designer, prop designer, and background designer. He has worked as a designer on projects for: Hulu, Cartoon Network, Springhill Company, FOX Sports, and FUSE. He believes that there is healing in storytelling, and that it is the job of creatives to contribute to that cause.

© 2023 Rourke Educational Media

All rights reserved. No part of this book may be reproduced or utilized in any form or by any means, electronic or mechanical including photocopying, recording, or by any information storage and retrieval system without permission in writing from the publisher.

www.rourkebooks.com

PHOTO CREDITS: cover, page 1: Illustration based on photograph by Damir Sagolj/REUTERS/Newscom, page 20: Bob Daemmrich/Polaris/Newscom

Quote source: Gabby Douglas & Michelle Burford. *Grace, Gold & Glory: My Leap of Faith*. Zondervan, 2012.

Edited by: Hailey Scragg
Illustrations by: David Wilkerson
Cover and interior layout by: J.J. Giddings

Library of Congress PCN Data

Gabby Douglas / J.P. Miller
(Leaders Like Us)
ISBN 978-1-73165-287-4 (hard cover)
ISBN 978-1-73165-257-7 (soft cover)
ISBN 978-1-73165-317-8 (e-book)
ISBN 978-1-73165-347-5 (e-pub)
Library of Congress Control Number: 2021952192

Rourke Educational Media
Printed in the United States of America
01-2412211937